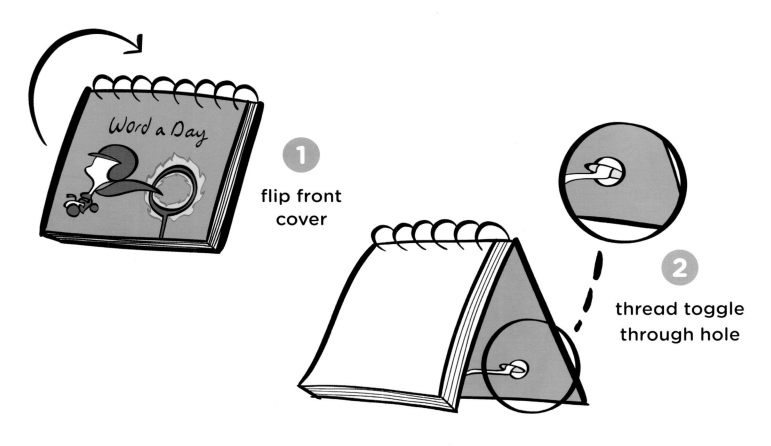

1 flip front cover

2 thread toggle through hole

Now, place the book on a surface, learn a word a day, and get r-r-ready for school.

Get started!

Get to know your Word a Day

Words with this icon are epic! They were chosen to challenge and inspire your child.

Words with this icon are Mrs Wordsmith's words for social-emotional development. The orange heart highlights words related to emotions, creativity, communication, and collaboration.

Words with this icon contain common phonemes. Scan the QR code on these pages to hear the correct pronunciation of the sound. This simple technology makes phonics fun and easy to learn at home and in the classroom.

inspire

/ire/

to make someone excited to do something

Books **inspire** Armie to go on adventures.

mrswordsmith.com

adventure words

QR Code

This feature allows you to hear how words are pronounced. Simply scan the QR code with the camera on your smartphone or tablet! Some devices will require a QR scanner to do this - these can be downloaded free from your app store of choice. If you are having trouble, you can find more detailed instructions at mrswordsmith.com

Phonics guide
to help you sound out the words

Vowel Consonant	/a/	/e/	/i/	/o/	/u/
	sad	empathy bread	invent	opposite	brush
/oi/ destroy point	/ou/ shout frown	/er/ smirk shower urgent	/air/ fair share bear	/or/* fork snore door	/aw/* draw exhausted
/ae/ play make paint	/oo/ short cook push	/oo/ long moody include few blue	/igh/ nightmare hide pie cry	/ee/ feet dream believe hungry these	/oa/ lonely soak toe
/ire/ inspire	/ar/ hard				
/f/ family different phone	/l/ learn silly	/m/ mistake shimmer climb	/n/ ruin funny know	/r/ repeat sorry write	/s/ secret messy police
/v/ volunteer love	/z/ amazing puzzled	/sh/ shampoo	/th/ soft thirsty	/th/ hard slather	/ng/ starving
/nk/ think	/b/ breath blubber	/k/ comfort break tricky	/d/ discover	/g/ gulp giggle	/h/ habit
/j/ jealous energy	/p/ problem happy	/qu/ quiet	/t/ tense	/w/ wait where	/ch/ cheerful watch

*/or/ and /aw/ sound the same in British English, but differ In American English.

You can help your child learn words!

Make learning words a daily habit

Set up your stand on the kitchen counter or dining table and talk about the words during mealtimes.

Sound out the word

Do this together. It helps children develop awareness of the correspondences between letters and sounds (phonics). See previous page for details.

Talk about the illustrations

Nothing develops children's thinking and language more than meaningful conversations with adults.

Don't skip the easy words

They help learners unlock harder synonyms. For example, **eat** unlocks **devour**.

Prepare them for school and beyond

Our words are curated around topics such as problem solving, creativity, hygiene, and emotional awareness.

Mrs Wordsmith is dragging word learning into the 21st Century

We think harder, and work smarter, to give kids the words they need to change the world.

Vocabulary has always been the best indicator of academic success. But in a world that is moving more rapidly than ever before, the way we teach kids words needs to keep up.

At Mrs Wordsmith, we believe in putting kids back at the heart of word learning. That's why we use Hollywood visuals to keep kids coming back for more, and data to curate the words that are relevant to today's fast-changing world.

We want to empower kids to become the designers, inventors, and leaders of tomorrow.

That means that kids not only need to learn rich, precise vocabulary, they need to learn words that develop creativity, social and emotional skills, and original thinking.

Words that help them find positive solutions to problems that don't even exist yet.

Words that help them inspire attitudes that make the world a fairer, more tolerant, and happier place.

We think harder, and work smarter, to give kids the words they need to change the world.

Find out more at mrswordsmith.com/research

Meet the Scooties

They'll help you scoot to the top of the class!

Grit

Bogart

Yin & Yang

Shang High

Brick

Plato

Oz

Bearnice

Armie

eat

/ee/

to put something in your mouth, chew, and swallow it

Oz **eats** spaghetti for dinner.

mrswordsmith.com

hungry

/ee/

how you feel when you want to eat

Yin feels so **hungry** that she points at her mouth.

mrswordsmith.com

starving

how you feel when you really need to eat
Grit is **starving** so he almost eats Plato's tail.

mrswordsmith.com

/ng/

thirsty

/th/

how you feel when you want a drink
Grit feels so **thirsty** that he will drink anything.

mrswordsmith.com

eat, sleep, and laugh words

dehydrated

when you feel weak because you haven't had enough water
Brick gets **dehydrated** in the hot weather.

mrswordsmith.com

nibble

/b/

to take tiny bites of something
Grit **nibbles** a delicious bone.

mrswordsmith.com

eat, sleep, and laugh words

gulp

/g/

to swallow a lot all in one go

Bearnice **gulps** an entire pool.

mrswordsmith.com

devour

to eat quickly or hungrily

Plato **devours** the whole pie.

mrswordsmith.com

tired

/ire/

when you haven't got any energy left
Oz is too **tired** to have fun on the swings.

mrswordsmith.com

eat, sleep, and laugh words

drowsy

/ou/

when you feel like you are about to fall asleep
Yin and Yang are **drowsy** after drinking the milk.

mrswordsmith.com

eat, sleep, and laugh words

exhausted

/aw/

when you are very tired and worn out
Shang High spills his juice because he is **exhausted**.

mrswordsmith.com

eat, sleep, and laugh words

sleep

/ee/

what you do when you shut your eyes at night to rest
Grit **sleeps** deeply.

mrswordsmith.com

snore

/or/

to make a snorting or grunting sound while you sleep
Bearnice **snores** so loudly that she keeps Bogart awake.

mrswordsmith.com

sleepwalk

/aw/

to get up and walk about in your sleep
Oz **sleepwalks** across her bedroom.

mrswordsmith.com

eat, sleep, and laugh words

laugh

what you do when you find something funny

Yin and Yang **laugh** constantly.

mrswordsmith.com

/l/

giggle

/g/

to laugh in a silly way

Plato and Bearnice **giggle** when they get covered in paint.

mrswordsmith.com

cackle

to laugh in a loud, wild way

Oz **cackles** when she finishes her evil plan.

/l/

eat, sleep, and laugh words

funny

/n/

something that makes you laugh
Grit wears a **funny** disguise.

mrswordsmith.com

eat, sleep, and laugh words

silly

ridiculous or nonsensical
Armie does something **silly** to make people laugh.

mrswordsmith.com

/ˈ/

hysterical

so funny you can't contain yourself
Foot tickles make Bearnice **hysterical**.

mrswordsmith.com

dream

/ee/

to close your eyes and imagine a whole other world

Oz **dreams** about winning a prize.

mrswordsmith.com

curious

when you really want to find out more about something

Plato is **curious** about the shell.

mrswordsmith.com

imagine

/i/

to use your mind to see the world completely differently

Grit **imagines** he is fighting a huge dragon.

mrswordsmith.com

discover

/d/

to find something new or unexpected

Shang High **discovers** Bogart under a rock.

mrswordsmith.com

draw

/aw/

to create a picture by making lines or marks

Yin and Yang **draw** a tiger in the sand.

mrswordsmith.com

creative words

write

/r/

to put letters or words on a page
Grit **writes** on the board.

mrswordsmith.com

paint

to create a picture with paint

Plato **paints** a picture.

mrswordsmith.com

/ae/

sculpt

to create a new shape out of something like stone or clay

Oz **sculpts** a statue of herself.

mrswordsmith.com

build

to put things together to make something new
Armie, Oz, and Bogart **build** a sandcastle.

mrswordsmith.com

/b/

fix

/x/

to put something back together again

Yin and Yang **fix** the broken vase.

mrswordsmith.com

adjust

to move or change something slightly

Shang High **adjusts** the temperature of the shower.

mrswordsmith.com

creative words

make

/ae/

to create or produce

Brick **makes** the best juice.

mrswordsmith.com

invent

/i/

to make or think of something new

Armie **invents** a flying machine.

mrswordsmith.com

creative words

design

to plan to make something

Oz **designs** a teddy bear.

mrswordsmith.com

cook

/oo/

to get food ready for eating

Grit **cooks** a meal.

mrswordsmith.com

concoct

Yang and Brick **concoct** a milkshake.

mrswordsmith.com

different

not the same as the others

Oz is **different** from the others.

mrswordsmith.com

unusual

Plato rides an **unusual** bike.

mrswordsmith.com

unique

Brick finds a **unique** flower.

mrswordsmith.com

opposite

completely different in every way

Bearnice and Bogart are in **opposite** moods.

mrswordsmith.com

/o/

hard

/ar/

something that is not easy

Armie finds the **puzzle** hard.

mrswordsmith.com

effort words

difficult

something that you find really hard

It's **difficult** for Bearnice to pull the sword free.

mrswordsmith.com

tricky

/k/

something that takes a lot of skill and practice

Shang High finds juggling **tricky**.

mrswordsmith.com

tough

something that is difficult and takes a lot of effort

Armie's training is **tough**.

mrswordsmith.com

/t/

confused

when you don't understand or you can't think clearly

Grit is **confused** by the complicated signs.

mrswordsmith.com

baffled

/f/

when you feel like something doesn't make any sense
Yin and Yang are **baffled** by the stranger who looks like them.

mrswordsmith.com

muddled

when everything is mixed up and the wrong way around

Armie feels **muddled**.

mrswordsmith.com

effort words

puzzled

/z/

when you can't work out how something happened
Plato is **puzzled** when he finds a sausage in a banana peel.

mrswordsmith.com

effort words

practice

doing something again and again so you get better at it

Armie has a lot of **practice** making paper boats.

mrswordsmith.com

habit

/h/

something you do often without having to think about it

Grit makes a **habit** of brushing his teeth.

mrswordsmith.com

effort words

repeat

to do something again

Yin **repeats** Yang's skating pattern.

mrswordsmith.com

/r/

fail

to try to do something and get it wrong

Shang High **fails** to put on his hoodie properly.

mrswordsmith.com

/I/

try

/igh/

when you make an effort to do something

Yin and Yang **try** to catch a star.

mrswordsmith.com

effort words

effort

when you really try to do something

Shang High makes a big **effort** to blow out the candles.

mrswordsmith.com

/f/

effort words

struggle

/s/

something that is difficult to do

The tug-of-war between Oz and Armie is a **struggle**.

mrswordsmith.com

push

/oo/

to keep going even when things get tough

Brick **pushes** on even though he is tired.

mrswordsmith.com

problem

something that has gone wrong and needs fixing

Plato has a **problem** when he runs out of toilet paper.

mrswordsmith.com

/p/

solution

a way to fix or solve a problem

Brick finds the **solution** to the puzzle.

mrswordsmith.com

mistake

something that goes wrong by accident

Plato makes a **mistake** and puts the record in the dishwasher.

mrswordsmith.com

challenge

Grit likes the **challenge** of climbing the wall.

mrswordsmith.com

effort words

messy

when everything is mixed up and out of place

Grit's room is very **messy**.

mrswordsmith.com

/s/

sloppy

/p/

when someone is careless or messy

Brick is a **sloppy** eater.

mrswordsmith.com

clean or messy words

dirty

Yin and Yang make the laundry **dirty**.

mrswordsmith.com

/d/

jumbled

/j/

when things are mixed up or not in the right order

Oz's shoes are **jumbled**.

mrswordsmith.com

wash

to make something cleaner

Yin and Yang **wash** themselves.

mrswordsmith.com

/w/

polish

/sh/

to make something shinier

Plato **polishes** his bill.

mrswordsmith.com

clean or messy words

soak

to leave something in water

Bearnice **soaks** her hair.

mrswordsmith.com

/oa/

shower

/er/

to wash yourself under running water

Plato sings while he **showers**.

mrswordsmith.com

clean or messy words

gargle

to wash your mouth and throat

Oz **gargles** every morning.

mrswordsmith.com

slather

/th/

to spread something thickly

Bogart **slathers** lotion all over himself.

mrswordsmith.com

scrub

/u/

Shang High **scrubs** the back of his neck.

mrswordsmith.com

clean or messy words

urgent

/er/

when you really need to do something

Oz has an **urgent** need for the toilet.

mrswordsmith.com

clean or messy words

relief

the good feeling you get when something unpleasant stops

Armie feels **relief** when he gets to the potty.

mrswordsmith.com

clean or messy words

unroll

to unwrap or unwind something

Yang **unrolls** the toilet paper.

mrswordsmith.com

flush

/sh/

to clear the toilet with water

Oz **flushes** the toilet.

mrswordsmith.com

shampoo

/sh/

to wash your hair with special hair soap

Bearnice **shampoos** her hair.

mrswordsmith.com

brush

/u/

to neaten your hair by running a brush through it

Grit **brushes** his fur.

mrswordsmith.com

clean or messy words

untangle

/a/

to get the twists and knots out
Shang High **untangles** his hair.

mrswordsmith.com

rinse

to wash something with water to get rid of the soap or the dirt

Armie **rinses** his body.

mrswordsmith.com

/r/

wear

/w/

to have clothes on your body

Oz **wears** new clothes.

mrswordsmith.com

truth

something that is real and true

Bearnice tells the **truth** about breaking the vase.

mrswordsmith.com

/th/

lie

to say something that is not true
Yang **lies** about taking the cookies.

mrswordsmith.com

fib

to tell a lie about something that isn't important

Armie **fibs** about being bitten by a shark.

mrswordsmith.com

exaggerate

to pretend something is more important than it is

Grit **exaggerates** how much his knee hurts.

mrswordsmith.com

trust

to believe in someone or something

Brick **trusts** Armie to catch him.

mrswordsmith.com

/u/

honest

when you are truthful and people can trust you

Oz is **honest** and gives Brick the money that he dropped.

mrswordsmith.com

fair

/air/

when something is right or honest
Grit splits the cookie in half to be **fair** to Bogart.

mrswordsmith.com

naughty or nice words

sincere

when you show your true feelings

Plato gives Bearnice a **sincere** apology.

mrswordsmith.com

naughty or nice words

mean

when you are unkind or unfair to other people

Armie is **mean** to Shang High.

mrswordsmith.com

nasty

when you are very bad or unpleasant to others

Plato is **nasty** when he steals Brick's lunch.

mrswordsmith.com

cruel

when you do something hurtful on purpose

Yin is **cruel** to Yang.

mrswordsmith.com

selfish

when you only think about yourself and not others
Oz is **selfish** and takes most of Bogart's cake.

mrswordsmith.com

kind

/k/

when someone is nice and does nice things

Yang is **kind** when she helps Shang High reach the leaves.

mrswordsmith.com

sensitive

when someone feels everything very deeply

Grit feels **sensitive** when his plant dies.

mrswordsmith.com

considerate

when you do something for someone else out of kindness

Plato is **considerate** so he helps Bogart cross the road.

mrswordsmith.com

sympathetic

when you understand how somebody feels and you comfort them

Brick is **sympathetic** when Armie's glasses break.

mrswordsmith.com

awesome

when something is amazing or incredible
Shang High's star-surfing is **awesome**.

mrswordsmith.com

amazing

/z/

when something is surprising or astonishing
Oz's trick is **amazing**.

mrswordsmith.com

impressive

when something is really good or awesome

Plato can fit an **impressive** number of cookies in his mouth.

mrswordsmith.com

extraordinary

when something is incredible or very unusual

Bogart shows **extraordinary** strength.

respect

to treat others with appreciation and behave politely

Oz **respects** the rules.

mrswordsmith.com

/t/

easygoing

when you feel relaxed and nothing bothers you

Brick is **easygoing** so he lets Yang sleep on him.

mrswordsmith.com

accepting

when you let people be whoever they want to be

Plato and Bearnice are **accepting** of Bogart.

mrswordsmith.com

tolerate

to put up with things that you don't like

Bearnice **tolerates** having her hair pulled.

mrswordsmith.com

zen words

feel

to experience something

The film makes Armie **feel** sad.

mrswordsmith.com

/ee/

relate

to understand someone because you have things in common

Grit can **relate** to Shang High's broken leg.

mrswordsmith.com

pity

a feeling of sadness or sympathy for another person

Oz feels **pity** for Bogart.

mrswordsmith.com

/p/

empathy

the ability to understand other people's feelings

Shang High feels **empathy** for the tree.

mrswordsmith.com

calm

when you feel still and relaxed
Grit stays **calm** despite the bees.

mrswordsmith.com

relax

when you take it easy and rest
Bearnice **relaxes** in her hammock.

mrswordsmith.com

/x/

zen words

breathe

to fill your lungs with air and let it out

Yin and Yang **breathe** fresh air.

mrswordsmith.com

balance

to stand without wobbling or falling over

Brick **balances** on his surfboard.

mrswordsmith.com

zen words

listen

to pay attention when someone speaks

Yin and Yang **listen** to Bogart's story.

mrswordsmith.com

understand

to know how something works

Bearnice **understands** how to tie her shoelaces.

mrswordsmith.com

focus

Plato **focuses** on the test.

mrswordsmith.com

concentrate

to think very hard about something

Brick **concentrates** so that he doesn't knock over the tower.

mrswordsmith.com

think

/nk/

what your brain does all the time

Bearnice **thinks** about where to put her block.

mrswordsmith.com

---

zen words

learn

to find out more about something

Armie **learns** to ride a bike.

mrswordsmith.com

/l/

reflect

to think about things that have happened

Grit **reflects** on his life.

mrswordsmith.com

thoughtful

when you take time to think about other people

Shang High is **thoughtful** so he keeps Plato dry.

mrswordsmith.com

zen words

fun

/n/

enjoyment, entertainment, or pleasure

Bearnice is having a lot of **fun**.

mrswordsmith.com

adventure words

carefree

/air/

when you are not worried about anything
Plato feels completely **carefree**.

mrswordsmith.com

adventure words

spontaneous

Armie goes for a **spontaneous** swim.

mrswordsmith.com

adventure words

surprising

/ng/

when something is shocking or unexpected

Yin always finds Yang's tricks **surprising**.

mrswordsmith.com

passion

a strong liking or love for something

Shang High has a **passion** for painting.

mrswordsmith.com

intense

something done with great effort

Yin and Yang have an **intense** staring contest.

mrswordsmith.com

energy

the ability to be active

Oz has enough **energy** to bounce all day long.

mrswordsmith.com

adventure words

enthusiastic

when you are very excited to do something

Brick is an **enthusiastic** fan of Plato.

mrswordsmith.com

risky

when something could go well or it could go badly

Plato's decision to press the button is **risky**.

mrswordsmith.com

/r/

harmful

when something causes hurt or pain

when something causes hurt or pain
Bogart accidentally breathes in the **harmful** car fumes.

mrswordsmith.com

/h/

adventure words

dangerous

when something is not safe

Yang should not bite the wire because it is very **dangerous**.

mrswordsmith.com

adventure words

play

to have fun in a game

Yin, Yang, and Brick **play** hide and seek.

mrswordsmith.com

/ae/

explore

/or/

Yin and Yang **explore** the ocean.

mrswordsmith.com

adventure words

seek

/ee/

to look for something

Shang High **seeks** the truth.

mrswordsmith.com

climb

/m/

to go up or get to the top of something

Oz **climbs** up the rope.

mrswordsmith.com

chase

to hurry after something and try to catch it

Grit **chases** his tail.

mrswordsmith.com

adventure words

lead

to have others follow you
Brick **leads** the mice.

mrswordsmith.com

guide

to show people the way

Grit **guides** his friends.

mrswordsmith.com

influence

to change the way other people act
Oz **influences** her friends.

mrswordsmith.com

inspire

/ire/

to make someone excited to do something

Books **inspire** Armie to go on adventures.

mrswordsmith.com

scared

Oz is **scared** of being so high up.

mrswordsmith.com

/d/

safe and scared words

spooked

how you feel when something scary surprises you

Yang is **spooked** when she sees the spider.

mrswordsmith.com

jittery

when you feel nervous and can't relax

Plato is a **jittery** flyer.

mrswordsmith.com

nightmare

/igh/

a scary or upsetting dream

Bogart has a **nightmare** about scary fish.

mrswordsmith.com

safe and scared words

shout

/ou/

to speak loudly or make a loud noise

Grit is very rude and **shouts** at Plato.

mrswordsmith.com

scream

/ee/

to make a long, high-pitched cry

Yin **screams** when she sees Bearnice.

mrswordsmith.com

shriek

to make a short, loud cry

Bearnice **shrieks** when she opens the box.

mrswordsmith.com

safe and scared words

squeal

/qu/

to make a long, high-pitched noise

Oz **squeals** when she sees the gift.

mrswordsmith.com

hide

to cover something up so that no one sees it

Yang **hides** under the rug.

mrswordsmith.com

/igh/

secret

something that you don't tell people

Armie has a **secret**.

mrswordsmith.com

bury

to put something in a hole and cover it

Oz **buries** her head in the sand.

mrswordsmith.com

disguise

to hide your face or dress up as someone else

Shang High wears a **disguise**.

mrswordsmith.com

hug

to squeeze someone in your arms to show you care

Yin and Yang **hug** Brick.

mrswordsmith.com

/g/

cuddle

/d/

to hold someone in your arms in a loving way

Grit **cuddles** his bone.

mrswordsmith.com

snuggle

/ˈsnʌɡ(ə)l/

to move your body into a warm, comfortable position

Oz **snuggles** with her teddy bear.

mrswordsmith.com

safe and scared words

huddle

/d/

to crowd closely together with other people

Everyone **huddles** together around the campfire.

mrswordsmith.com

safe

/ae/

to be free from harm or danger

Shang High feels **safe** because he is wearing lots of protective gear.

mrswordsmith.com

safe and scared words

secure

to be free from danger or risk

Armie feels **secure** because he is wearing lots of seat belts.

mrswordsmith.com

comfortable

Bearnice feels **comfortable** in her big, soft armchair.

mrswordsmith.com

harmless

something that isn't dangerous or likely to cause harm

Brick knows that the spider is **harmless**.

mrswordsmith.com

/s/

safe and scared words

friends

people who get along well and love each other
Oz and Bearnice are **friends**.

mrswordsmith.com

/f/

family

/f/

a group of people who love and take care of each other

Brick goes out for a walk with his **family**.

mrswordsmith.com

friendship words

team

/ee/

a group of people who work together to do something

The animals form a rowing **team**.

mrswordsmith.com

friendship words

ignore

to take no notice of someone or something

Oz **ignores** the sign on the beach.

mrswordsmith.com

exclude

to leave someone out

Grit and Bogart **exclude** Shang High from their joke.

mrswordsmith.com

neglect

to forget about something and stop looking after it

Oz **neglects** her plant.

mrswordsmith.com

reject

to strongly say no to something

Bearnice **rejects** all broccoli.

mrswordsmith.com

like

/igh/

to have a good feeling about something or someone
Grit **likes** ice cream.

mrswordsmith.com

love

/v/

to have very strong affection for something or someone

Yin and Yang **love** each other.

mrswordsmith.com

adore

to love someone and think they are very special

Bearnice **adores** Bogart.

mrswordsmith.com

obsessed

Armie is **obsessed** with his new video game.

mrswordsmith.com

friendship words

share

/air/

to do something with other people

Shang High **shares** a hotdog with his friends.

mrswordsmith.com

friendship words

include

/oo/

to let everyone join in

Bearnice **includes** Grit in movie night.

mrswordsmith.com

friendship words

together

when you do something with another person

The friends carry the fridge **together**.

mrswordsmith.com

friendship words

collaborate

to work together

Yin and Yang **collaborate** to build a snowman.

mrswordsmith.com

help

to make something easier for someone
Oz **helps** Brick by giving him a life ring.

mrswordsmith.com

/e/

friendship words

save

/ae/

to keep safe or rescue

Brick **saves** Yin and Yang from the tree.

mrswordsmith.com

friendship words

fasten

/n/

to close or buckle securely

Brick **fastens** his seatbelt.

mrswordsmith.com

friendship words

comfort

/k/

to soothe someone or make them feel better

Plato **comforts** Armie.

mrswordsmith.com

friendship words

smirk

/er/

to smile in a mean way

Yang **smirks** when she steals Yin's teddy bear.

mrswordsmith.com

break

/k/

to separate into pieces with force
Armie **breaks** his pencil.

mrswordsmith.com

destroy

/oi/

to completely ruin something
Grit and Bogart **destroy** the sofa.

mrswordsmith.com

tantrum words

ruin

to spoil or destroy
Bearnice **ruins** the cake.

mrswordsmith.com

/n/

shatter

/er/

to break into lots of little pieces

Oz **shatters** the mirror.

mrswordsmith.com

moody

/oo/

when you feel sad one moment and happy the next

Plato feels very **moody**.

mrswordsmith.com

tantrum

when someone is crying, shouting, and out of control
Brick has a **tantrum** and bangs his fists on the ground.

mrswordsmith.com

grumpy

/ee/

when you are in a bad mood

Armie feels **grumpy** in the morning.

mrswordsmith.com

tantrum words

frustrated

when you feel annoyed and can't stand it anymore

Oz is **frustrated** when the cards collapse.

mrswordsmith.com

cry

/igh/

what you do when you're sad and tears fall from your eyes

Yin and Yang **cry** about the spilled milk.

mrswordsmith.com

sob

/b/

to cry noisily with loud gasps

Bearnice **sobs** until her head hurts.

mrswordsmith.com

blubber

/b/

to cry uncontrollably and loudly

Plato **blubbers** for so long that his house fills with tears.

mrswordsmith.com

tantrum words

wail

/ae/

when you get upset and cry out with a long, high noise
Armie **wails** when his toy is taken away.

mrswordsmith.com

frown

/ou/

a sad expression with your eyebrows pushed down

Oz has a **frown** on her face.

mrswordsmith.com

tantrum words

pout

/ou/

to stick your lips out in a moody way

Armie **pouts** and crosses his arms.

mrswordsmith.com

tantrum words

scowl

to frown in an angry or bad-tempered way

Grit **scowls** at the camera.

mrswordsmith.com

sulk

to be quiet, and grumpy, and mope about
Brick **sulks** when he doesn't get his way.

mrswordsmith.com

sorry

when you feel sad or regretful

Yin said **sorry** for accidentally hitting Grit with a baseball.

mrswordsmith.com

/r/

apology

a way of showing that you are sorry

Brick makes an **apology** to Armie for dropping his ice cream.

mrswordsmith.com

forgive

to stop feeling angry towards someone

Bearnice **forgives** Yang for eating her cookies.

mrswordsmith.com

/v/

tantrum words

regret

when you feel bad and wish you hadn't done something
"I **regret** eating so many doughnuts," says Plato.

mrswordsmith.com

excited

when you feel a lot of enthusiasm and energy

Grit is **excited** by what he sees on TV.

mrswordsmith.com

impatient

when you can't wait for something to happen

when you can't wait for something to happen
Bogart is **impatient** to eat pizza.

mrswordsmith.com

feeling words

eager

when you really want to do something

Shang High is **eager** to eat ice cream.

mrswordsmith.com

feeling words

thrilled

when you are very happy and excited

Armie is **thrilled** when the rocket takes off.

mrswordsmith.com

feeling words

hurt

how you feel when someone does something mean

Oz feels **hurt** because her doll is torn.

mrswordsmith.com

feeling words

upset

/u/

how you feel if you are sad or worried about something

Bearnice is **upset** because her skateboard is broken.

mrswordsmith.com

feeling words

jealous

/j/

how you feel when you want something that someone else has

Yin is **jealous** of her sister's trophy.

mrswordsmith.com

feeling words

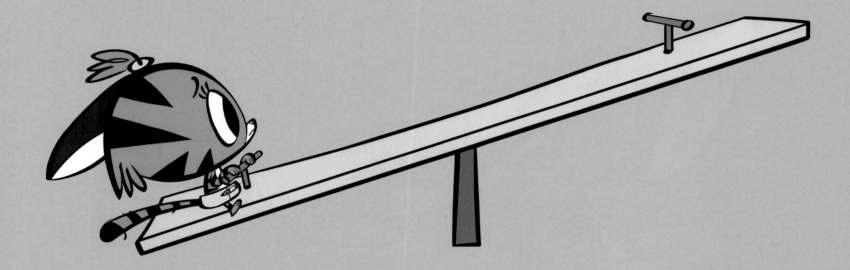

lonely

/oa/

when you feel alone and sad

Yang is **lonely** on the seesaw.

mrswordsmith.com

feeling words

sad

/a/

when you feel unhappy

Yin and Yang are **sad** when they lose their balloon.

mrswordsmith.com

feeling words

heartbroken

when something makes you very upset and sad
Oz is so **heartbroken** that she falls to the floor.

mrswordsmith.com

feeling words

miserable

when you feel very unhappy or uncomfortable

The cold bath makes Yin and Yang **miserable**.

mrswordsmith.com

disappointed

how you feel when something isn't as good as you expected

Oz is **disappointed** with her birthday present.

mrswordsmith.com

angry

Oz is so **angry** that she might explode.

mrswordsmith.com

annoyed

Armie is **annoyed** with Brick for being silly.

mrswordsmith.com

feeling words

disapproving

when you think something is wrong and you show it

Bearnice **disapproves** when Yin draws on the wall.

mrswordsmith.com

feeling words

fuming

when you feel lots of anger building up inside
Plato is so angry that he is **fuming**.

mrswordsmith.com

happy

Brick and Grit feel **happy** in the pool.

mrswordsmith.com

/p/

cheerful

/ch/

when you are in a very good mood

Yin and Yang do a **cheerful** dance.

mrswordsmith.com

feeling words

blissful

when you are completely happy in every way

Bearnice feels **blissful** on the grass.

mrswordsmith.com

feeling words

elated

when you are so happy you feel like you could fly
Shang High feels **elated** after making a friend.

mrswordsmith.com

nervous

/er/

when you are scared or unsure about something

Armie is **nervous** about going down the slide.

mrswordsmith.com

first day at school words

worried

when you are afraid that something will go wrong

Bearnice is **worried** that Bogart will fall and hurt himself.

mrswordsmith.com

anxious

Oz is **anxious** about getting into the pool.

mrswordsmith.com

tense

/t/

Grit is **tense** because he wants to win.

mrswordsmith.com

first day at school words

shy

Brick feels **shy** at parties.

mrswordsmith.com

/igh/

timid

when you don't feel brave or confident

Shang High feels **timid** when he meets new friends.

mrswordsmith.com

quiet

/qu/

when there is very little noise and nothing to disturb you

Plato finds a **quiet** spot to relax in.

mrswordsmith.com

first day at school words

embarrassed 🔊

when you feel ashamed and just want to hide
Grit feels **embarrassed** when his trousers rip.

mrswordsmith.com

first day at school words

speak

/k/

to say something out loud

Yin and Yang **speak** into the string telephone.

mrswordsmith.com

contribute

to give something or help out

Grit **contributes** money to charity.

mrswordsmith.com

volunteer

/v/

to put yourself forward to do something

Oz **volunteers** to answer the question.

mrswordsmith.com

first day at school words

join

to become part of a group or start doing something

Oz **joins** the water fight.

mrswordsmith.com

confident

when you feel sure of yourself and what you can do

Oz is **confident** that she can fly.

mrswordsmith.com

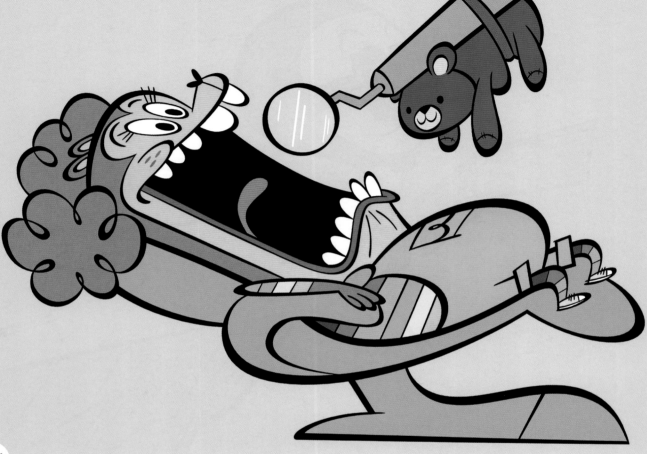

brave

when you are ready to do something that scares you

Bearnice is **brave** when she visits the dentist.

mrswordsmith.com

first day at school words

bold

when you are ready to take risks or do risky things

Armie has **bold** plans.

mrswordsmith.com

courageous

when you are not scared away by danger

Brick is **courageous** when he saves people.

mrswordsmith.com

wait

to pause until something is ready

Brick and Plato **wait** to use the toilet.

mrswordsmith.com

/w/

patient

Bearnice is **patient** as she waits for a cupcake.

mrswordsmith.com

polite

when you behave in a respectful way

Oz is very **polite** to her friend.

mrswordsmith.com

cooperate

to help someone or work together

Yin and Yang **cooperate** to get the cookies.

mrswordsmith.com

first day at school words